Saving Netty

Rescuing an American White Pelican

Bruce Thomas

Illustrated by
Kayla Swedberg

Saving Netty: Rescuing an American White Pelican

Copyright © 2020 Bruce Thomas

All rights reserved. This book or any portion thereof may not be reproduced or used in any manner whatsoever without the express written permission of the author except for the use of brief quotation in a book review.

Printed in the United States of America

First Printing, 2020

ISBN: 978-1-7343741-0-0 (Print)
ISBN: 978-1-7343741-2-4 (Hardcover)
ISBN: 978-1-7343741-1-7 (eBook)

For ordering information please email SavingNetty@gmail.com

Book Formatting by Becky's Graphic Design, LLC
BeckysGraphicDesign.com

Illustrations by Kayla Swedberg
TheBrandHuntress.com

Sketches by Elyse Dutch

DEDICATION

This book is dedicated to our Creator and his Son Jesus Christ. The God-given talents that we all possess will allow you to do great things in this world.

My family is the greatest gift I will ever receive. They are a treasure that is beyond measure. My wife is the counterbalance that I need daily. My children are a gift whom I am charged with raising in The Word so that they may go out and make the world a better place. As our children grow, we can ready them for this world so that they may lead by example through love and encouragement.

The world is a beautiful place. As we take it all in and appreciate its beauty, we can all make it a better place for those who learn from our daily actions and will follow in our footsteps.

Rachel, Presley and Rhett, I love you!

I hope you and your family enjoy the story and the wonderful illustrations.
Thank you Kayla and Elyse!

Every spring, American White Pelicans fly from their warm winter home around the Gulf of Mexico back to their summer home in Canada.

In the summer, Canada is lush and green with lots of lakes full of fish. Pelicans can fly thousands of miles each year.

The pelicans will stop along the way to eat fish and rest for their next flight. Migrating from Gulf Coast to Canada requires a lot of stops along the way.

Cedar Creek, on Old Hickory Lake, is one of the pelicans' favorite places to stop and rest. Cedar Creek is filled with lots of small fish that pelicans love to eat.

American White Pelicans have a large orange bill that they use to scoop up fish from the water. Pelicans often hunt fish together as a family. A pelican can eat up to four pounds of fish per day!

Presley is a girl who lives close to Cedar Creek. She loves to spend time on the lake swimming, fishing, and playing with her family on the water.

She and her brother, Rhett, have lots of fun!

One day Presley saw the pelicans arrive and was very happy to see them. She loved the way they flew together and landed on the water with their feet skimming on the surface.

Presley noticed one of the pelicans was swimming all by itself. "Pelicans stick together," she thought. "I wonder why that one is swimming all alone?"

Presley watched the pelican as it swam closer. She noticed something was wrong. The pelican looked very tired and hungry. Presley noticed something strange on its big orange bill.

The pelican had some red plastic netting stuck around his bill. The pelican, whose name was Netty, could not open his bill to scoop up fish and could barely get a drink of water.

Netty had not eaten in days and was very hungry. Netty's feathers were also very dirty. Pelicans use their bill to clean the dirt off their beautiful white feathers.

Netty was not a very happy pelican…

Presley went to her father and asked him to look at the pelican. "See Daddy, look at his bill," she said.

Presley's father saw the red netting and asked Presley, "What do you think we should do?"

"Let's help him, Daddy; let's help him!" Presley said. So that is what they set out to do.

"How do you catch a pelican?" she asked. Presley's father had never caught a pelican before but they had to try.

They tried to get Netty to come to them with bread and catch him in a net, but that only works with ducks.

They tried to lasso Netty with a rope, but that only works with cows and cowboys.

Finally, Presley and her father decided to try something different, something that would require teamwork.

Presley's brother watched for Netty to make sure he did not swim out of the marina. Presley's father got on a paddle board and paddled out to Netty. He tried to get Netty to swim into an area where they could catch him by hand and remove the plastic netting from around his bill.

Netty swam around and around the marina avoiding Presley's father. Pelicans are very good swimmers.

Finally, Netty got tired and swam into an empty boat slip. Presley tried to grab Netty, but he was too big. American White Pelicans are four feet tall.

Netty swam under the boat dock and into the next slip. There was a large boat in that slip and Netty was too big to swim between the large boat and the boat dock.

Presley and her father gently grabbed Netty by his big orange bill and removed the plastic netting.

Presley helped Netty swim past the big boat and back out into the marina.

Netty was free and he could open his big orange bill again!

Netty was very pleased but he was still very hungry and too weak to fly.

Presley and her father went up to the restaurant and asked for some raw cod fish fillets. The chef asked, "What for?"

"We are going to feed a pelican!" answered Presley.

Presley and her father broke the cod fish into small pieces and fed them to Netty. Pelicans like fish as much as ducks like bread.

Netty ate all of the cod fish and gave them a nod as if to say "thank you."

Presley was very happy that she and her family were able to help Netty.

Presley's father was happy too. "Good job! I am very proud of you and your brother!" he said.

Netty was now a very happy pelican. He could hunt fish with his family, drink water, and clean his beautiful white feathers.

Presley watched Netty swim to the island where he climbed up on the shore and began cleaning his feathers. After all of that swimming around, Netty was very tired.

With a full belly of fish, Netty took a long nap.

The next morning Presley and Rhett spotted Netty out hunting fish again with his family. This made them very happy and proud of what they accomplished together.

They saved Netty!

A few days later Netty and his family took off and continued north to their summer home in Canada. Presley saw the pelicans flying north and said, "I hope we see Netty again next year."

"We will," answered Presley's father. "We will."

I am a Husband and Father who takes every day with my family as a gift. I try and make the most of each day and lead with love and encouragement. I am a pilot by trade. When not spending time with my family, I serve at church as a leader and learn something new every week.

Am I perfect? Not even close! Am I persistent? You better believe it. I try to stack one good decision upon another to one day be an example of success.

My life's new motto is "From Here," living life looking forward.

-Bruce Thomas

CPSIA information can be obtained
at www.ICGtesting.com
Printed in the USA
LVHW072118270421
685768LV00001B/1